KATHLEEN PARTRIDGE'S
Golden Thoughts

To

....

From

....

Jarrold Publishing, Norwich

TO A FRIEND

A golden thought has just begun
Where flowers blossom in the sun
And rivers sing to those who pass
While shadows lean against the grass.

Then I would wish a friend like you
Another friend as good and true
To share the road of life's design
With humour and a love divine.

Graceful Ivelet Bridge straddles the
River Swale near Muker, Yorkshire

The imposing yet majestic abbey at Tewkesbury,
Gloucestershire

FAR AWAY PLACES

Turn back the page, the page of time
To the olden days of maypoles and mime
To a white horse carved on an old green hill
With a mason's art and a carpenter's skill.

To beautiful churches in ancient glory
And stained glass windows that tell a story
Turn back the page, recapture grace
And try to live at a quieter pace.

Beautiful stained glass windows in the Lady Chapel,
Ely Cathedral

ONLY A PETAL

Only a leaf in the morning dew
Or hole in the fence where a rose climbs through
The song of the sea or the sunset's kiss
Life is worth living for this.

Only the smile of the child next door
Or news from a friend on a distant shore
Though the rest of the day has gone amiss
Life is worth living for this.

Only a petal pale and pink
With memories sweet to form a link
With past or present times of bliss
Life is worth living for this.

The exquisite oxalis deppei

Some magnificent roses are grown at the Royal National Rose Society Gardens, St. Albans

This old fashioned clock graces the Town Hall in Guildford

TOLL OF TIME

Time takes its toll
And those we love grow dearer with the years
Of no avail are past regrets
Life has no time for tears.

Live and laugh and help each other
Whether working or at leisure.
To be happy, loved and needed
Is life's greatest source of pleasure.

Time stands still at Owlpen Manor, Gloucestershire

SUNBEAMS

If all the golden sunbeams
Could be gathered in to spend
With all the loving thoughts and deeds
When day was at an end

And tied with strings of laughter
On wings of wonder born
They'd beautify the eventide
And bless tomorrow's dawn.

A delightful view over the fields towards Hawes,
North Yorkshire

The sun sinks behind the cliffs of Iona, Strathclyde

Waters ripple gently by the Island of Mull

ANOTHER DAY

Old cares are like the morning mist
Before the rising sun
But it is true, the blue shines through
Before the day is done

And then the fears of yesteryears
Go rolling down the lane.
Another day, smiles on its way
And life begins again.

Carbis Bay, St. Ives – an ideal setting for a summer holiday

RIVER OF LIFE

Peace and the flowing river of life
Offer us hope and a little song
A sense of comfort and ease from strife
Whenever the toils of life are strong.

And over the hills where the views are kind
A feeling of freedom is waiting there
A solace of heart and soul and mind
Out on the grass in the open air.

Time to cool off.
River Stour, Shillingstone,
Dorset

The elegant gardens of Polesden Lacey in Surrey

SOMEBODY'S GARDEN

Someone planned this garden
From the beauty in his soul
And kept his spirits joyful
As he worked towards this goal.

Breathing sunshine from the flowers
And wisdom from the leaves
To offer comfort to the sad
And peace to the heart that grieves.

Traditional thatched cottages at Pitch Green,
Buckinghamshire

BLOSSOMING SMILE

Nature's loveliness would pall
If flowers had no scent at all
For beauty lifeless stands apart
Without the fragrance in the heart.

A maiden might a goddess be
Perfect in grace and symmetry
Yet stand unnoticed for a while
Without the beauty of a smile.

A colourful profusion of cineraria

The magnificent blooms of the lavatera

A stirring way to start the day, north of the Border

TUNE OF THE DAY

A joyful manner of living
Is a tune for the day to start
The pleasure in doing and giving
Brings peace to the happy heart.

With courage for daily duty
And patience when problems arise
Thankful for bounty and beauty
Living in ways that are wise.

The wild beauty of Glentrool Forest,
Dumfries and Galloway

Time for a nap for this yellow labrador and puppy

OUR DOG

He is more than a pet. He is more than a friend.
He's a reason for living on which we depend.
With his head on one side and his paw held aloft,
Our firmest reproval grows suddenly soft.
He meets us, he greets us, enslaved from the start,
When he nuzzles our hand as he tugs at our heart.

A beagle's pleading gaze is hard to resist

DREAM COTTAGE

We picture a country cottage
Set in a country lane
Scented with old fashioned flowers
And sheltered against the rain.

Old timbers and quiet windows
With a beautiful garden view
Where the shadows play in the evening
And the morning sun filters through.

It's a dream that can make us happy
When we live in a busy part
Dreaming the dream of 'Our Cottage'
And keeping the hope in our heart.

Cottages in the unspoilt village of Waterstock, Oxfordshire

Roses almost overwhelm this cottage in Noss Mayo, Devon

The harbour at Polperro, Cornwall, provides boats with welcome shelter

WISDOM OF THE WAVES

When the ships are safe in harbour
And the boats are anchored tight
When the sun gleams on the water
There is not a fairer sight.

The lonely heart is comforted
The troubled mind set free
As if the cares of all the world
Were sailing out to sea.

Casting cares to the wind

FRIENDSHIP

Old friends are like old shoes
They are so fitted to the years
They know our highest efforts
And discern our secret fears.

They've walked with us and waited
When we aimed for better things
Through embarrassment or glory
Poor as paupers, proud as kings.

And though for various reasons
Shoes wear out and friendships end
We lose part of our lives
Each time we quarrel with a friend.

Time to stop and admire the scenery

A woman's best friend. . .

A magnificent country house in Great Dixter, Northiam, Sussex

FOR THE LOVE OF A ROSE

Is it an angel's secret tears
In the heart of a rose when the dew appears?
Or the scroll that curls at the petal's edge
That talks of love and a lover's pledge?

Or is it the perfume, deep and sweet
Where the loveliest hours of the summer meet
To lighten the heart and to ease the woes
And make us live for the love of a rose?

This superb rose is called 'Superstar'

WORLD PROBLEMS

When happy do not close your eyes
To other nations woes and sighs
Though healthy, not too proud to see
Another's disability.

Let pageantry be fine and wise
With music set to sympathise
While wealth and comfort serve to stress
World problems and a child's distress.

On parade in Hyde Park, London

The Houses of Parliament — a fine example of
neo-gothic architecture

GLINT OF GOLD

In every humdrum day
There is a little glint of gold
A purpose in the living
That is lovely to behold.

A reason for existence
In the dark — a glowing ember
That lights the dullest duty
With a moment to remember.

A glorious sunset marks the end of another day

It's a duck's life at Earlswood Lakes in Surrey

Stately Diss Church in Norfolk is an impressive sight

WHERE GOD IS

Upon the hill a Norman tower
Among the trees a spire
And cuddled down amid the town
A lych gate to admire.

A cathedral in the city
Or a meeting house of prayer
Each village street, or green retreat
Proclaims that God is there.

St. Gregory's, Norwich — a favourite place for a
midday pause

THE OLD AND THE NEW

From the old church organ music floats
To the lazy lapping of little boats
With perky sails and painted hulls
And over it all the squeal of gulls.

Above the harbour, bustling about
The world comes in and the world goes out
By way of a bridge — the latest kind
Created and built by a master mind.

New and old bridges contrast
effectively at South Queensferry,
Lothian

SLEEP TIGHT

In between the dimpled hills
Along a leafy lane
A pretty cottage slumbers
In the sunshine and the rain.

The roses ramble round it
Where the apples trees bend low
And good folk live in harmony
While fashions come and go.

The place where love is waiting
In the way that God designed
When someone mentions 'Home'
This is the place that comes to mind.

This most charming cottage is situated in Oxwich,
Glamorgan

Roses embellish this delightful English country house

Autumn leaves pave the way through woodland in Surrey

THE WANING YEAR

Now dripping leaves weep for the loss of Spring,
And days that danced till dusk are darkening.
The wind awakes, more boisterous from repose
And bares the heart of every dying rose.
The golden leaves grow frail and loose their hold,
Then mother earth receives their wealth of gold.

Admiring the view – Reigate Hill, Surrey

MEN AND BOATS

The world a sorry place would be
Without a river running free
Between the meadows and the hills
With water for the farms and mills.

And pastures green lack something too
Without a river running through
With dipping ducks and swans afloat
Where men keep young who sail a boat.

Sailing on the River Yare at Coldham Hall, Norfolk

Peace and quiet at Letheringham Mill in Suffolk

Northleach in Gloucestershire is the setting for this
tranquil view

TO LIFT THE HEART

Think of a lovely landscape
If ever you droop with despair
Picture the perfumed pathways
The dells and the arbours there.

Sit in a shady corner
Or lounge on a sunny slope
Where nature brings you contentment
And God will offer you hope.

Upper Slaughter in Gloucestershire — the very heart
of England

WAKE UP AND SMILE

This is the day to wake and say
Happy the heart that is merry in May.
Gather contentment as you pass
Green and serene, the colour of grass.

To be awake when blossoms break
And sunbeams smile for someone's sake
The views so free, so much to see
The best of summer yet to be.

Blossoms at their best near Sissinghurst in Kent

The River Stour flows gently through Canterbury

Taking a stroll around Great Budworth, Cheshire

REMEMBERING

Never a day runs to an end
Without some kindness from a friend.
Without remembering the name
Of one we love who stays the same.

To doubt the love of such a one
Would be to disbelieve the sun
A lack of faith, that stays awake
Doubting that the dawn will break.

There's room to breathe on this beach at Iona, Strathclyde

Dramatic cliffs rise above the bay at Porthcurno, Cornwall

HIGH HOPES

May your hopes run clear
As the waters of life
And high as the shining blue
And all the love
That you gave to life
Come back on the tide to you.

May the colour of dreams
That dry your tears
Be gold as the morning glow
Bringing a blessing
Along the years
To the dearest people you know.

A panoramic view near Abbotsbury, Dorset

AUTUMN TINTS

Out on the common the bracken is turning
From green and yellow to bronze and gold
The flames of autumn are bright and burning
Over the hills where the clouds unfold.

And there will be fragrance from autumn showers
And morning sunshine to gleam and glisten
Scattering light on the blazing flowers
Where man may prattle and God will listen.

The face of the changing seasons in the Yorkshire Dales

Golden reflections in the River Dart at Holne Bridge, Devon

A spectacular sunset at St. Brelades, Jersey

SUNSET

A golden shaft of sunlight
Makes a pathway to the sea
As if an angel host
Had walked into eternity

A blessing and a beauty
Never quite so fine before
That lights the sky at sunset
From horizon to the shore.

And then we know that God is good
Whatever man may do.
A sign of love shines up above
And hope is born anew.

The calm waters of Loch Eil, Highlands

DINNERTIME

No sweeter sight to ease the soul
Than meadows with a horse and foal
Trampling where they love to be
Near by the shelter of a tree.

Slender forelocks flashed with white
Where yellow buttercups are bright
Tender eyes and velvet nose
Whereon the wind of heaven blows.

Who roams the countryside will know
The secret sights that do not show
But to the country lover's soul
What dearer than a horse and foal?

Following in mother's footsteps

Mare and foal enjoying the good life

The green and pleasant landscape of Naunton,
Gloucestershire

ON THE TIDE OF LIFE

In the ripple of a river
In a house beneath a hill
May you find the hidden secret
That is life, come good, come ill.

With humour in the common round
And joy in simple pleasures
Wherever life may lead you
May you gather countless treasures.

Foaming waters of the Afon Teifi, Cenarth, Dyfed

ONLY A DAY

Create if you can a lovelier thing
In sheen and shade than a butterfly's wing
So many colours brightly blended
Into a life so quickly ended.

Only a day of joy and duty
To give the summer so much beauty
A simple friendship with a flower
Packed into a shining hour.

A Vanessa butterfly displays its colourful wings

Hovering over an astor is the small tortoiseshell butterfly

FOR OLD TIME'S SAKE

Think golden thoughts
And send out gentle blessings
Offer a prayer
Each time you look above.

For kindly people
Found in pleasant places
Remember them, for old time's sake,
With love.

The haunting scenery of the Yorkshire Dales

ISBN 0-7117-0347-7 © Copyright Jarrold Publishing 1988. Reprinted 1989, 1992. Designed and produced by Parke Sutton Limited for Jarrold Publishing, Norwich. Printed in Portugal.